MW00604464

fresh wood
v.2

Greg Asbury
Judy Smith Asbury
Margrit Lehmann Beltran

Mitra
PUBLISHING GROUP
Sierra Madre, California

Detail "Curve Front Cabinet"

Fresh Wood v.2
© 2006 Mitra Publishing Group

first printing

All rights reserved.
No part of this book may be reproduced, stored or distributed in any form or by any means, electronic, mechanical, photocopying, recording, or otherwise (except as permitted by Sections 107 and 108 of the U.S. Copyright Law and except by reviewers of the public press) without prior written permission of the publisher.

Principal photography by Greg Asbury.

Design and layout by Verna Loughran Baz and Greg Asbury.

Additional photos by Gary Michael, Exposures Ltd. (AWFS® Fair trade show photography).
Ashley Hilton's Dinner Table photo by Seth Tice Lewis.
Ana Luisa Franco's Mommy & Me Seating photos by Steven Heller.
Photos of Eidelbaub Jr and Polyidol provided by Scott Grove.
Donated photos from Mike Ferguson, Ana Luisa Franco, Matthew Harrell, Matthew Hieb, Natalie Hunsaker, Ben Johnson, James Kearl, Dan Overby, Kirsten Skinner, Katie Stanchak, Rachel Winderweedle and Jonathan Nazareth Zabala.

Published by Mitra Publishing Group

225 North Lima Street, Suite 6

Sierra Madre, California 91024

United States of America

ISBN-13: 978-0-9654003-7-4
ISBN-10: 0-9654003-7-9

Printed in China through Palace Press International.

With contributions by
Steve Ehle
Nancy Fister
Scott Grove
Helen Kuhl

Detail "Horizon"

I drove out of the Strip, still bathed in neon, well before dawn to the Valley of Fire some 50 miles northeast of Las Vegas. Few visitors actually come to this remarkable valley, but it seemed a perfect location to take photos of some of the extraordinary entries in the student design contest. With them loaded safely in the backseat, I sought out their connection to the natural world.

Light comes up early and dramatically in this desert. It paints an extraordinary landscape in the ochre and chocolate hills that surround the manmade oasis of Las Vegas. Sunrise comes quickly—pinkish, flat, warm, probing. Within the "magic hour" between dawn and day, sunlight becomes baking, incinerating, brilliant white. Far outside the neon and the seething crowds this is a world of intense natural beauty.

We think of manufactured chairs, machined surfaces, inlaid tables as the built environment. Contemporary design seems invented and functional apart from the organic natural forms that have shaped our history. But it just couldn't be farther from the truth. Bringing the chairs and tables—whimsical sculptures—into this setting seemed oddly out of place but at the same time connected to its natural forms. Design imitates life. Life needs design—form with function.

Nature is like a fine art collector in this harsh realm preserving its artwork in dessicated time. I carried my props through the red rock formations of sandstone once at the bottom of an inland sea. Thrust into hills and carved by all of nature's forces. There were many reminders of our ancestors. Petroglyphs scratched into the rock faces capturing so many forms and designs. It was an amazing sight to realize that our distant ancestors had the gift of vision. For the sake of design itself and the sheer exhuberance of communication to other humans, they had incised their own visions into the red rock. Designs were everywhere! Communications delivered. Frozen on the rock faces. Burnt into desert varnished stone. Indeed this was the connection I was searching for.

Many of the student design entries in this book echo nature and organic forms found in this desert. A turned bowl-shaped table with laminations reflected the layers of the rains that had come to the desert the day before. The marvelous bowl floating on its curved wooden tripod was reflected in a pool of catch water. As I photographed it, the pool of rainwater in the stone basin was rapidly evaporating, leaving striations in the rocks as it had done over many eons. The natural mirror was gone in a few hours but the table froze this force of nature and captured its intricate patterns within.

Las Vegas seems like a world apart. And it is in many ways—the glitter, the neon, the pumped water, the choreographed light ballet in front of Bellagio, the Stratosphere's view from the needlelike tower. But Las Vegas, in all of its shapes and overdriven glare, had also been created by the same magic that was woven into so many of the forms and shapes of the marvelous furniture and embedded by the visions of the young designers who wrought these creations .

It may seem out of place to see the natural wonders of our surroundings against the posed furniture pieces. But in a way it seemed so natural to include them in this book because it is the unseen joint, the hidden half haunch tenon, the play of wood grains in exquisite marquetry that is reflected in our natural world. Treasures waiting to be discovered, waiting to reveal their secrets in an early morning dawn out in the desert.

Greg Asbury

Detail "Stayin' Alive"

CONTENTS

THE STUDENT DESIGN COMPETITION

The Association of Woodworking & Furnishings Suppliers® (AWFS®) created the Student Design Contest in 1999 as part of an industry education initiative adopted that year by its Board of Directors.

One of the goals of that initiative focused on ways to create a better bridge between industry and education. There was (and still is) a large gap between the two. High school shop classes are still in decline and support for technical vocational programs continues to wane in many areas. Where it does exist, "woodshop" curriculum has often not advanced with the industry, nor recognized how technical wood manufacturing has become. Teachers were feeling isolated and there was no ready source to identify woodworking programs and allow them to connect with each other, let alone with industry.

The First AWFS® Student Design Contest

It was in this environment that the Student Design Contest was born. From the beginning, it was decided that this contest must include high school students, which distinguished it from other student woodworking contests of the time. AWFS® sought to recognize high school students and teachers by encouraging them to participate, acknowledging that high school is the key time for making career-setting choices. At about the same time the contest came into being, another fledgling program, WoodLINKS USA, was getting off the ground. WoodLINKS is an industry-education partnership that brings wood technology programs in schools together with local industry to build the core curriculum. A standard skill set is taught and students are tested at the end of the program, producing highly desirable and employable graduates. The Student Design Contest gave the WoodLINKS teachers motivation and an avenue of expression for the talents being developed through this program. It is no surprise that most of the high school entries are coming from WoodLINKS schools. In addition to the new encouragement for high schools, the contest has ignited interest and participation from technical schools, community colleges and postsecondary design, architectural and engineering programs across North America.

Myles Multhauf
Eight-Drawer Mission Style Dresser

The first Student Design Contest premiered at the 1999 AWFS® Fair in Anaheim, California, drawing a modest number of entries. That number doubled for the 2001 contest and doubled again in 2003. The 2005 submissions reflected a 40% increase from a widening number of schools and geographic regions across the United States and Canada.

AWFS® wanted to make the contest as accessible as possible to all students at accredited schools. Therefore there is no entry fee, and once selected as a finalist, AWFS® pays to ship the entries to the AWFS® Fair for display and final judging. The association also underwrites much of the cost for both students and teachers to attend the Fair, providing hotel accommodations and a travel allowance. Teachers and students are encouraged to meet and exchange information with other schools, as well as view the hundreds of exhibit displays of the latest industry innovations and make connections with industry leaders.

Another feature of the contest is the support for school wood technology programs. The school of the student who captures the Best of Show award receives a check for $2,500 for the school's program.

Sam Maloof Creates Best of Show Sculpture

In 2001, renowned wood artist Sam Maloof was commissioned to create a special sculpture for the Best of Show winner for each biennial show. A coveted feature of the contest, this sculptural award is designed by the internationally revered woodworking artist, and when his schedule permits, he attends the show and presents it himself. While Sam maintains an air of gentle humility, students are near speechless to have his full attention focused on their projects. It is a special moment at the trade show's Recognition Reception, when all finalists and their teachers are honored and presented their awards.

Providing the Leadership

Setting the parameters of the contest is the AWFS® Student Design Committee, a sub-committee of the Education Committee. Playing a leadership and guiding role for the contest, Duane Griffiths, Education Manager for Stiles Machinery, Inc., has served as the Committee Chair since the inception. For each contest, a new committee comprised of industry volunteers is created. The Committee is charged with setting policy and rules, making recommendations for revisions and for appointing a panel of judges—drawing from various aspects of the industry including design, manufacturing, retail, education and trade publications.

Changing Perceptions

Through programs like the Student Design Contest, AWFS® hopes to build awareness of the importance of the relationship between industry and education. In addition, the contest helps to change outdated perceptions of the career opportunities and skill levels in the woodworking industry. School programs need to reflect the changes and advancements caused by technology and a global economy, as well as bring awareness of the existence of substantial job openings offering competitive salaries for skilled workers in a diverse range of career paths. A sampling includes high tech machinery operation and repair, computer controlled machinery operators, sales, international trade, teaching, forestry, milling, hardware, machinery and product design, as well as R&D related to coatings, finishings and innovative wood products that combine with metals, plastics and solid surfaces.

The profile of the students enrolled in career technical education classes also needs to move away from outdated, unflattering characterizations. The 2003 Contest finalists included two high school valedictorians and two salutatorians. In 2005, another winning entry came from a high school valedictorian. Entrants are coming from high schools and technical schools as well as prestigious universities across North America. The caliber of the work completed by these students exceeds all expectations and continues to "dazzle" the trade show attendee audience.

Inspiring Work

While the caliber of work submitted in the contests had been impressive from the beginning, the 2003 entries, at both the high school and college level, astounded exhibitors, attendees, industry personnel and the trade press. There was a tremendous buzz at the show surrounding the contest, which resulted in the publication of *Fresh Wood*, a full color art book showcasing all the finalists' work with numerous photographs and personalized project descriptions.

Sarah Puchosic
Links

Skylar Davis
The EasySit Mission Recliner

3

Pictured L to R: *Julia Beamish, Charles Monaco, Jr., Nancy Fister, Scott Grove, Brian Dyches, Gary Rogowski, Craig Bren, Michelle Olsen, Anatole Burkin*

Judges
Michelle Olsen and Scott Grove examining an entry

THE DESIGN CONTEST JUDGES

The judges represent five areas of the industry to lend a variety of perspectives to the judging process. Those include manufacturing, retail, design, education and trade press. The 2005 student design judging panel included:

DESIGN
Scott Grove
Designer, Sculptor, Owner of Concept Grove
(Rochester, New York)

Charles Monaco, Jr.
Design Director at Furniture Design Studios, Inc.
(Huntington, New York)
President of American Society of Furniture Designers (ASFD)

EDUCATION
Julia Beamish
Professor of Housing at Virginia Tech (Blacksburg, Virginia)

Gary Rogowski
Craftsman and Director of The Northwest Woodworking Studio
(Portland, Oregon)

MANUFACTURING
Craig Bren
Vice President of Sales for Tuohy Furniture Corp.
(Chatfield, Minnesota)
Technical Consultant for Tuohy Forest Products

RETAIL
Brian Dyches
President/CEO of Atmospheric Group
(Laguna Niguel, California)

Michelle Olsen
Interior Designer with Kubala/Washatko Architects
(Cedarburg, Wisconsin)

TRADE PRESS
Anatole Burkin
Executive Editor for *Fine Woodworking* magazine
(Newtown, Connecticut)

Helen Kuhl
Editor in Chief of *Custom Woodworking Business* and *Closet* magazines (Lincolnshire, Illinois)

Teachers across the U.S. responded with excitement about the book and began incorporating it into classroom use. Cliff Durand of Dakota High School told us, "I have shown it to my students and they are inspired by it—a feat hard to do with high school students." Mark Smith of Shiloh High School (whose students participated in 2003) commented, "Students, teachers, administrators and parents have all come down to see the book. They couldn't believe how nice all the projects looked. It helped everyone see that their students/children were among an elite group."

In 2005, 160 entries came in from ten high schools and twenty-three postsecondary schools. Eighteen of those schools were participating for the first time. A total of 58 pieces made the cut as finalists, chosen for display at the July AWFS® Fair in Las Vegas.

The trade show's new location in Las Vegas has added to the level of excitement for participants. The vibrant city and its magnificent desert backdrop lend awe and inspiration to many young people who have not yet ventured far from home. The size and scope of the show's 900 exhibitors, demonstrations and education programs (the education programs are offered free to the contest students and teachers) are all a learning experience created by the contest.

The contest currently offers first place and honorable mention awards in several categories. Two special awards include the Best of Show and the People's Choice. It is conceivable that one entry can capture a First Place, the Best of Show and the People's Choice awards—and it happened in 2001 to Steve Lacey of Cerritos College in Southern California (now an instructor at the college) and in 2005 to Joshua Williams of Rockingham Community College in North Carolina.

With *Fresh Wood v.2*, you can glimpse for yourself the impressive level of work that is being produced, gain information on the schools with dynamic instructors and wood programs, as well as learn about WoodLINKS USA.

Nancy Fister
Director of Education Programs, AWFS®

John Maher
Contour

More information on the Student Design Contest can be found at www.awfs.org

Detail "Bridge Table"

Detail "Treble Rocker"

Reviewing the Work
by Scott Grove

It is always a privilege to attend an AWFS® Fair. To be invited to review and judge the 2005 Student Design Contest was truly an honor. When I was first asked, I jumped on the chance. I've got 25 years in the fine furniture business, participated in many trade shows myself, viewed a wide range of work, mentored students at many levels, written and spoken about design and marketing, and I thought—this will be a piece of cake and a free trip to Vegas! Needless to say I hadn't a clue what I was in for.

The first packet of preliminary scoring material arrived weighing in at least ten pounds, and I found myself a bit overwhelmed as I sat on my living room floor sorting through this pile of creative wonder.

Clearly the pieces that were photographed well stood out, crisp renderings were even more influential, and clean mechanical and AutoCAD drawings showed a good sense of construction intent. I found the lengthy descriptions interesting and thoughtful, but also mind-numbing mostly because of the sheer volume.

(Tip Number One for next year's contestants: 3D renderings work best since, understandably, many pieces were not completed or photographed well. The best design with precise craftsmanship may not make the cut if conveyed poorly in a photograph or drawing.)

With this in mind, I attempted to judge on all the criteria, focusing on design, productivity and other discernable measures. At this level, design was clearly the dominant judging factor, but I wasn't sure how to consider the finish or clean-cut dovetail by looking at a photo. This anticipated one-night affair and my free trip to Vegas was turning into a week of late nights, piles of categories, great work, better work, great good work and better good work. I carefully selected the top pieces and off they went, done, which was what I thought was the most difficult part. Little did I know that I had a full day of intensive scutization ahead of me.

Once arriving in Vegas and seeing the furniture on display, I started to think about all the work that had to be completed, photographed, crated

Whitney Bradford
Phyllis

Curtis Chilton
Night Stand

and shipped on time to this surreal wonderland. I empathized with what the finalists must have gone through, as I don't believe Furniture Shipping 101 is included in today's academic offerings.

Bright and early all the judges gathered for the first viewing. We were given our instructions, handed another ream of scoring sheets and off we went, working intently and independently.

A few surprises occurred. The first was how strong the high school work appeared. Strong design and acceptable craftsmanship from these students was certainly giving some of the college-level work a run for the money. I did have much higher expectations for the older students.

The weakest link in many pieces clearly was a poor finish, which may be a result of lack of facilities and/or academic focus. Unfortunately this stood out as I sighed with disappointment and sympathy. The entrants with hand-oiled works seemed to have realized this dilemma, so their pieces were soothing to look at and to touch. I noticed many of the judges caressing the work, too.

Another very astonishing missed detail was the lack of final cleaning. (Tip Number Two: After 400 hours of work, spend five more minutes and clean your piece before shipment.)

Scott Grove, principal designer for Concept Grove Incorporated (CGI) creates unique, contemporary art. Grove has been commissioned by major corporations such as Eastman Kodak and Bausch and Lomb, and has created public art for the City of Rochester, New York—In addition to his work for designers, architects and private collectors. He has won numerous awards and honors including a DuPont prize for innovative use of materials.

Polyidol

Eidelbaub Jr.

Although some pieces apparently went terribly wrong with assembly, for example a few had severe veneer bubbling (which obviously didn't show up in the photographs), I seem to accept this for the high schoolers and even congratulated them for attempting the process.

I was also lenient on questionable structural inadequacies on pieces that obviously pushed the design envelope. A few pieces really hit the boundaries and tested the waters, which I found very refreshing. In high school and college study it is the time to test these waters—sink or swim is very commendable—jump in as opposed to playing it safe.

I did however, also enjoy many of the traditional category pieces, and felt the sensitive design proportions were right on.

A few other interesting observations came to light. Firstly, the obvious retro design flavor flashing back to my early years in the 60's & 70's. Groovy baby! Though dated, it is certainly one of my favorite styles. I just wish I had saved my bell-bottoms.

Secondly, and more profoundly, is the concern for social and economic issues. The consideration for materials yield, recycled and green materials should be commended. The use of system construction (ready-to-assemble and knock-down), and considering cultural context in which the piece would be used was enlightening and encouraging. Although 'special needs' was a category, many works impressively demonstrated thoughtfulness and sensitivity in these areas.

Despite minor defects, some dusty work and poor finishes, the most impressive characteristic was design; the risks that were taken were the most exciting aspect of the show to me. Now is the time for students to take risks, because when one enters the real world, aesthetic risks have to be weighed against financial ones.

Being accepted into this national level show is obviously a great honor and I was honored to participate. I commend AWFS® and sponsors for committing to the development of our future craftsmen and designers.

Rachel Winderweedle
Walnut Chest

Joshua Nickolds Williams
Newport Block Front Desk
Newport Corner Chair

Detail "Pedestal Table"

THE IMPORTANCE OF TAKING A RISK

One of Scott Grove's favorite themes for students is about taking risks. "This is the time to take risks, push the envelope and experiment. Take risks with esthetics, structures and materials. Do it now, while you're a student," he implored. "In the real world you've got to make a living. You can't often afford the freedom to experiment; you've got to sell your work and making mistakes affects the pocketbook."

Grove has good reason to believe in experimentation. Two large deviations from his standard work have now become signature pieces: his Idol Series of fiberglass sculpture and his Inlaid Gem furniture series. But he was not able to explore those ideas until well into his career, when he found ways to incorporate that experimentation into existing projects.

Grove admonishes instructors to help their students experiment. "Hopefully the instructor rewards his/her student for experimenting. You can't know where the line is until you cross it. You don't know how thin you can make the wood until it breaks. You don't know how far you can push the structure until the joint fails. You don't know what new material can do until you work with it."

Students should not be so concerned about creating a finished work of art, according to Grove. "A student can experiment with many things, learn from all of them and not necessarily make it into a finished piece."

To illustrate his point, Grove told of a project with a recent intern in his studio. "I asked him to make a dozen drawers, each time using a different construction technique. We kept time studies and when he was done, we tested them all—so we knew what worked best, what wouldn't work, and the cost associated with it."

"In hindsight," Grove remarked, "I wish I had taken more risks when I was living in my mother's basement. I regret not exploring more materials, more techniques early in my career."

Luckily for all of us, Grove has managed to experiment enough to produce award-winning innovative work that is displayed in the finest galleries, homes and offices.

"You don't know where the line is until you cross it..."

Detail "Quilted Blanket Chest"

Looking at the Future
by Helen Kuhl

Fifty-eight pieces. That's what it boiled down to—58 finalists chosen from among 160 total entries in the 2005 student furniture design competition, sponsored by the Association of Woodworking & Furnishings Suppliers®. For those of us given the honor of being judges, it was the final step in the daunting task of choosing winners from among a wide variety of pieces, with styles ranging from sleek contemporary to time-honored traditional. It was a privilege to spend a day pulling out drawers, looking into cabinets, running hands over surfaces and just enjoying the visual impact made by attractive and, in some cases, highly inventive designs.

While the day was a time for judges to concentrate on the task at hand, in the end it also left time to realize that we were not just viewing the work of a few talented students, but also getting a glimpse into the future of the woodworking industry. How the American woodworking industry fares in the future, now more than ever, depends on today's students and the paths they choose.

The woodworking industry is an exciting, enriching and fulfilling segment of U.S. manufacturing. The times are not without their challenges for the industry, however, and one of the biggest is obtaining a dedicated, enthused and skilled work force to sustain it into the future. Participation in industry group meetings, speaking with industry leaders and hearing from individual shop owners constantly confirms for me the serious need for good employees that is felt at woodworking businesses of every size.

It is imperative that today's young people—tomorrow's potential employees—are aware of the vitality of the industry and career opportunities available, or there will continue to be a shortfall of workers that will weaken the industry. Woodworkers currently involved in the field realize how rewarding it is; the challenge is to ensure that today's students are cognizant of those benefits, too.

Emily Kale
Puzzle Me Pretty

Vitaliy Verbovskiy
Craftsman Curio Cabinet

Kirsten Skinner
Wine Rack

Having a venue such as the AWFS® competition to express their creativity and celebrate their skills is a wonderful step to encouraging young people to consider choosing woodworking as a career. It exposes them to the opportunities and the depth of job possibilities that exist. It also is a good forum for the participating schools to provide their local school boards with tangible proof that the woodworking industry is not only alive and well, but also thriving. That is a critical point to be made during times like the present, when many school programs are being closed.

The need for skilled woodworkers has far-reaching implications. Like many other industries, woodworking has entered a truly global arena and faces competition from manufacturers around the world. Some of them have distinct advantages due to lower labor costs and other factors. The U.S. industry must maintain its advantage by offering high quality, inventive styling and fast delivery, with the flexibility to adapt to rapidly changing consumer tastes and emerging trends. These are the factors that will continue to set the American industry apart, factors that other countries can't match. And to achieve those advantages requires skilled workers.

Today's woodwork manufacturers don't simply need bodies on the shop floor. They need capable employees that will keep the industry moving forward, which further underscores the importance of today's students to the future.

To see the enthusiasm and interest of those who participated in the AWFS® contest at both the high school and postsecondary levels is a very hopeful sign. Also a positive note is the level of skill and design creativity exhibited by this year's entrants. It was evident that the students had invested a great deal of time, thought and pride into their projects.

It also was a tribute to the excellence of their teachers and the woodworking programs in place at their schools. Student inspiration and development of skills start in the classroom, nurtured by dedicated and enthusiastic teachers. Fortunately, there are a host of strong teachers across the country, and there are great initiatives taking place, such as WoodLINKS, to bolster woodworking education in the U.S. These are the elements that must be in place for the industry to hold its own against global competitors. It requires everyone involved to be supportive and vigilant to ensure continued progress.

Finally, a tribute should be given to the students who won first-place honors in 13 categories for their outstanding work, as well as those who earned honorable mentions. As you leaf through this book and enjoy the skill and creativity evident in the winning projects, remember that you are looking at the early works of tomorrow's fine craftsmen and inspired designers. I wish them continued success as they put their talents to work and join a vibrant industry. In whatever capacity they decide to participate, they are sure to be a great asset.

Tighe James Smalley
Propeller Study Bench

Helen Kuhl has been an editor with Vance Publishing Corp. since 1988, serving as chief editor of Custom Woodworking Business since its inception in spring of 1991. She also was instrumental in the development of Closets magazine, which debuted in November 2003, and continues to serve as its Editor in Chief. Helen is a member of the Architectural Woodwork Institute's Development Council and the Education Committee of the Association of Woodworking & Furnishings Suppliers®. She also serves on the Advisory Committee of Fox Valley Technical College, Wood Technics Department, in Oshkosh, WI.

Ryan Wither | *RELAXATION*

RELAXATION stood out above many impressive projects at the 2003 AWFS® Student Design Contest. A modern and elegant lounger of metal, wood, and massage balls, RELAXATION impressed the judges with its outstanding quality in both construction and design. When Sam Maloof, renowned designer and woodworker, presented the Best of Show award, he remarked, "When I laid down it, I didn't want to get up again. That's good design."

Ryan Wither created RELAXATION when he was a graduate student at Savannah School of Design as part of his Master of Fine Arts thesis. Paul Basile, owner of Basile Studio in San Diego, saw the chair at the 2003 AWFS® Fair and decided to hire Ryan as lead designer for his custom line of furniture. There in California, Ryan honed his skills in high-end metalworking and furniture design.

A year later, Ryan and friend, Paul Lewin, started a new venture and Tivi Wear was born. A distinctive line of women's accessories, Tivi Wear combines their passion, charm and craftsmanship with stainless steel, supple leather, and exotic wood. Sadly, Ryan had to sell RELAXATION to help finance the new venture. Although disappointed, the investment paid off, and Tivi Wear is now featured in over 30 upscale boutiques across the nation, and has received publicity in esteemed magazines such as *Dwell* and *Lucky*.

2003 CONTEST WINNERS

Ashley Hilton | *Dinner Table*

In summer of 2003, Ashley Hilton had just graduated with honors from high school and had visions of a future in the furniture industry. Although so young, her credentials were already being tested. She had submitted two projects to the AWFS® Student Design Contest, which were selected as finalists. When all projects were displayed at the Fair, viewers couldn't help but notice the beautiful round dinner table exuding a warm elegance with its array of rosewood grain spreading out from a pinpoint at the center of the tabletop. The outcome was clear; the people voted and Ashley's Dinner Table won the People's Choice award.

When she graduated from high school, Ashley had also completed the WoodLINKS USA certificate and was awarded a scholarship from AWFS®, which is available to WoodLINKS graduates. Her WoodLINKS experience, as well as her success at the AWFS® student design contest, opened doors to meet people and make connections in the industry. In April of 2005, she went to Florida to attend a Woodworking Industry Conference (WIC) and speak on behalf of WoodLINKS. She also received considerable publicity for winning the People's Choice award, and together with being featured in *Fresh Wood: New Designers, v.1*, both her confidence and her credibility has grown.

Ashley is now in her third year of studies at Appalachian State University, pursuing a degree with a double major in Furniture Studies and Business. She is looking to own her own custom woodworking business and perhaps getting her Masters degree to teach.

Best of Show

People's Choice

Fine Woodworking
Craftmanship Award

Newport Block
Front Desk

Joshua Nickolds Williams | *Rockingham Community College*

Seeing early American furniture up close was the definitive moment for Joshua Nickolds Williams. It opened his eyes to the brilliant design and craftsmanship that marked furniture of the era.

"One of the required courses at Rockingham Community College Fine and Creative Woodworking Program is 'History of American Furniture'," Josh explains. "As part of the class we visited the Museum of Early Southern Decorative Arts in Winston-Salem, and each of us built a Queen Anne lowboy. Once I completed the class, I was hooked."

Ironically, Josh's math and engineering background gave him a particular appreciation of the furniture design, but he left that major after three years at the University of Georgia when he realized his interests lay elsewhere. "I wanted to be hands-on, to work with something physical. Advanced math and engineering were both oriented towards computers. I wanted to work with something real."

Researching his next educational and career move, Joshua remembered the time he spent with this father learning woodworking. The two spent

Joshua Williams receives awards and congratulations from Scott Phillips of American Woodshop, Rockingham Community College instructor Art Pentz, and Duane Griffiths, AWFS® Education Committee Chair and Education Manager of Stiles Machinery Inc.

one week each summer taking a woodworking class together, and Josh helped his father with various remodeling and hobby projects. This led him to the program at Rockingham Community College where his excitement grew as elements he had learned of woodworking and history from books he began to experience through the actual construction of furniture. The class and the museum trip sparked a passion that continues to grow.

Although his first class projects were contemporary in style, he had been attracted to the classic design, the integration of proportion, the curved lines and ornamentation befitting the wealthy landowners and businessmen in eighteenth century America. In particular, he favored the work of the Newport Rhode Island furniture makers renowned for their craftsmanship, and admired the work of the Goddard and Townsend Cabinetmakers as well as the modern construction

of Robert Emmet's twentieth century reproductions. While considering what he might make next in his class, he picked up some old Fine Woodworking magazines his father had given him. In a strange coincidence, an August 1980 issue published the month and year he was born, featured the Newport Block Front Desk with scaled drawings, as well as the techniques of Robert Emmet.

Using the information in the magazine as well as his own research, Joshua spent over 30 hours hand drawing a full set of plans for the massive desk. This process, though exhausting, helped him to visualize the challenging spots. "When I finished, I felt like I had already built this piece once."

Josh chose Black Cherry wood and carefully selected a log from a specialty hardwood dealer, Hearn Hardwoods. "The Mahogany that the early Americans used is not available today. I chose Black Cherry because of its close grain structure and sturdiness. I built this desk to last 300 years."

Josh started the desk in November 2004 and completed his finish just prior to the AWFS® Fair. He did most of hand carving at home because of limited time the Rockingham Community College shop.

"Hand carving the exterior shells and inner shells was the most difficult. Those took me about 75 hours to complete. But it is the part I love the

best—my first set of woodworking tools were hand tools. And although this was the fun part for me, I knew if I made a mistake it would change everything—I didn't have more wood or time to redo it."

The hardware for the desk came from Ball and Ball Hardware and includes six fully functional locks which had to be placed in exactly the right position, both for design and function.

Josh chose a shellac for his finish, keeping the tradition of the early American furniture makers. "It took a month for the shellac to harden enough to sand to a sheen. The finish will darken to a patina over time. Many people suggested I stain it for a darker color, but I prefer a new piece, rather than a true reproduction."

"Overall the design is what I appreciate most. I thought a lot about the tradition and the craftsmen when I made this. I had a sense of communing with the people and history of early America. I hope the original furniture makers would be happy and proud that their furniture is still being made."

Detail "Contemporary Dining Chair"

Detail "Propeller Study Bench"

Casework-Cabinets – Creative

Mike Ferguson, University of Kentucky . . . . .Male/Female Dresser

Renee' D. Shellhammer, University of Kentucky . . . . .skeleton-skin-transparency

Casework-Cabinets – Traditional

Joshua Nickolds Williams, Rockingham Community College . . .Newport Block Front Desk

Curtis Chilton, Fullerton College . . . . .Night Stand

Natalie Hunsaker, Brigham Young University . . . . .The Chicago

Jonathan Uecker, Fox Valley Technical College . . . . .Curve Front Cabinet

Chairs – Creative

Ben Johnson, Appalachian State University . . . . .Stayin' Alive

Matthew Harrell, Georgia Institute of Technology . . . . .Contemporary DiningChair

Chairs – Traditional

Joshua Nickolds Williams, Rockingham Community College . . . . .Newport Corner Chair

Tables – Creative

Kirsten Skinner, Miami University . . . . .Wine Rack

Dan Overby, Rockingham Community College   "My Feathered Friends"
                                                          Demilune Table

Tables – Traditional

Scott Price, Cerritos College . . . . Art Deco Inspired Console Table

Upholstered – Creative

Ana Luisa Franco, Art Center College of Design . . . . .Mommy & Me Seating

Upholstered – Traditional

Hamilton Trimm, Auburn University . . . . .Horizon

Special Theme – Special Needs Furnishings

Tighe James Smalley, Appalachian State University . . . . .Propeller Study Bench

Jonathan Nazareth Zabala, Art Center College of Design . . . . .Flex Shelf System

Team

Mathew Birtch and Jessica Lertvilai, Sheridan College . . . . .Flex Folding Stool

Male/Female
Dresser

My inspiration is to see how design relates to life. I want people to view my work and change their view of design.

This dresser is a combination of solid and void and the interaction between the two types of materials. The concept for this project was to give an understanding of how male and female roles are played in organizing space. The walnut is the masculine side where the male would place his clothes and the white oak would be the same for the female.

The casework is made of 3/4-in finished plywood and 1/2-in solid wood drawers. The drawers are made of solid walnut and white oak wood with fingerjoint construction. The drawer pulls are made to give a representation of the voids created in the connection between these two masses. The steel frame elevates the dresser to visually slim down the weight and provide a connection between these two masses. It is welded 1-in tubing and the pulls are 3/4-in steel tubing. The unit of 7 1/2 inches was used several times in the design of the piece.

Mike Ferguson

Mike Ferguson | *University of Kentucky*

Skeleton. Skin. Transparency. These are the contributing factors of the overall design of this entrance table. An entry table becomes a place to display, to collect, and to organize most everyday items—pictures, keys, unpaid bills and the important reminder, the note. With this in mind, the overall intent was to create a relationship with the very same object that interacts with this table, the human body.

The black skeleton of 18-guage tube steel becomes the dominating material, establishing stability and structure. Everything else becomes skin, and the organs (the internal components) in the deepest layer become visible through the transparent skin.

Transparency is introduced in different ways in this table. One is the use of 1/4-in glass, frosted to let the viewer catch a glimpse of blurred objects through the other side. The glass door slides on a track to cover no more than two bays at one time. Another material used is 1/2-in maple veneer wrap overtopping the skeleton, providing a place to hide and protect objects from the eye. And finally, the sheet metal perforated with 1/2-in squares is intended to give the viewer yet another perspective of the organs.

Reneé D.Shellhammer

Reneé D.Shellhammer | *University of Kentucky*

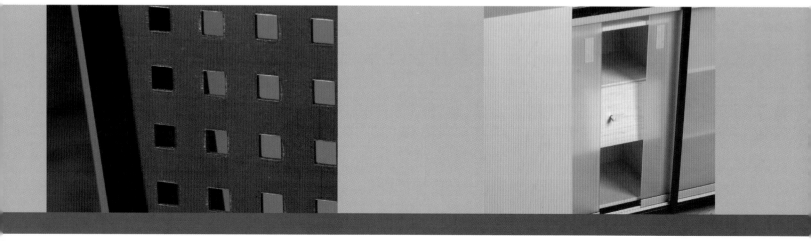

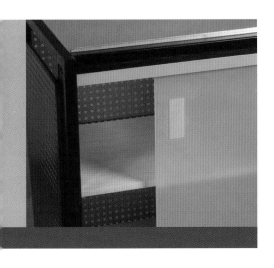

skeleton-skin-
transparency

Newport Block Front Desk

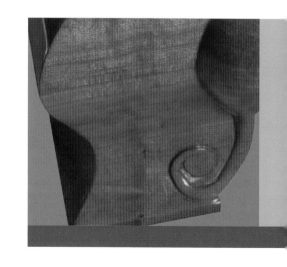

This desk is a reproduction of a portion of the secretary made for John Brown by John Goddard, which is the most expensive piece of American furniture ever sold at auction. The block front style of case furniture features alternately convex and concave shaping of the case front, and the Newport hallmark of deeply carved shells. The construction is based on the work of Robert Emmet.

I chose to build this desk from black cherry because it is an American hardwood and has a nice grain, density and working properties. I began with four air-dried consecutively-sawn 26-in planks from a substantial cherry tree. I dovetailed the main case components, including the 13 drawers. Drawer dividers and full dustboards were joined to the sides with sliding dovetails. The base moulding and feet were joined at the front corners with full blind dovetails. All dovetails were cut by hand.

I shaped the feet, drawer fronts and mouldings with hand planes, carving gouges and rasps. The most difficult and time-consuming part was hand carving the six shells on the desk lid and inside the gallery. A finish of shellac over oil brings out the beautiful grain and natural color of the cherry.

Joshua Nickolds Williams

Joshua Nickolds Williams | *Rockingham Community College*

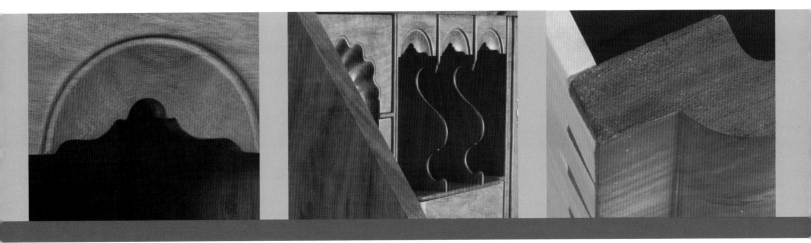

Night Stand

The inspiration for this project came from a dresser I have that exemplifies arts and crafts, and is one of several furniture pieces acquired by my grandfather during the depression as payment for his labor. This nightstand is a companion to that dresser.

The design challenges of this project were twofold: to balance specific desires and needs with space constraints, and to maintain the general proportions and decorative details from the dresser in a harmonious design.

The height and width of the half-width drawers at the top of the original dresser were nearly ideal for creating a bank of three drawers in the nightstand. I decreased the height of the top drawer to allow for the pullout shelf. I used solid quarter-sawn oak for the drawer fronts and bottom rail, as well as the stiles, rails and panels of the case sides. The drawer bottoms and back panel are Baltic birch. The pullout shelf is maple with white oak trim at the front. I commissioned a router bit to cut the unique design of the double beading on the drawer rails. The drawer knobs are reproductions of those on the original dresser.

Curtis Chilton

Curtis Chilton | *Fullerton College*

When I began the initial sketches for The Chicago, I had never touched a tablesaw, let alone understood the processes behind the biscuits, raised panels and mortise and tenon joinery I used.

As my first attempt at creating furniture, I wanted a simple, yet conservative and classy bed for my fiancé and I. Communicating uptown style, it was to portray by its stately appearance that it belonged in Mom and Dad's room. My fiancé added one more request—the ability to dangle his feet off the end of the bed.

The Chicago uses 16/4 cherry in the bedposts and top beams, as well as solid cherry paneling. The use of solid wood ties the piece to historically formal furniture. The hand-cut beveled glass adds a modern cosmopolitan twist. The arc at the headboard adds to the graceful aesthetic and is repeated at the lower (rather than the upper) portion of the footboard to ensure that it does not rise above the mattress.

My fiancé and I couldn't be more pleased with the final result. After the wedding, we will be moving to Chicago.

Natalie Hunsaker

Natalie Hunsaker | *Brigham Young University*

Traditional | Casework-Cabinets

The Chicago

I designed this curved cabinet with clean lines so that the wood itself would give the piece character. Wood is a natural material and including "defects" such as solid knots, bark pockets or worm holes in a piece of fine furniture only adds to the beauty of the final product.

I used steam bending and bent lamination to make the black walnut door rails and trim pieces. The black ash door panels were coopered by gluing them together and then shaping them with a CNC router. Sizing, building, and fitting the doors to the openings were the biggest challenge throughout the whole process. I began to enjoy the problem-solving part of this project. Many times I said,

"Here is what I want to end up with. Now how do I get there?" Then I would have to find the process or come up with another jig. The whole project required about 25 different jigs.

I like to design furniture that includes elements of construction or design features that would be considered traditional but with a more modern look. A number of my pieces have a similar look to Shaker furniture.

Jonathan Uecker

Jonathan Uecker | *Fox Valley Technical College*

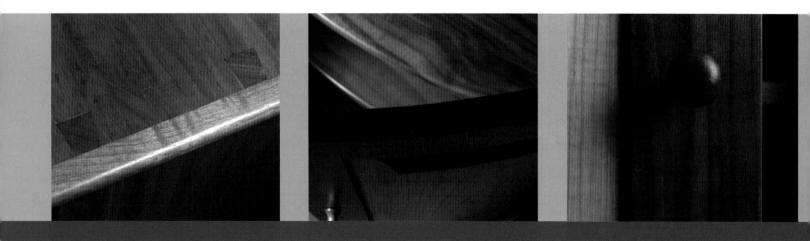

Traditional | Casework-Cabinets

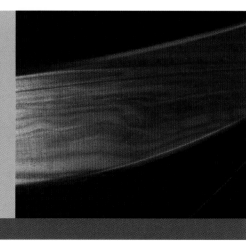

Curve Front Cabinet

Stayin' Alive

I wanted to create a stylized all-wood chair to rival the comfort of a padded chair by using the natural flex of the wood itself. I chose dowels because they allow the seat to conform to different people's lumbar curves and avoid creating any pressure points. The styling of the chair was centered on the legs and stretchers, which flare out to create a bell-bottom look (hence the name Stayin' Alive).

I chose mahogany for the frame because it bends fairly easily, and walnut for the dowels because it is strong and contrasts visually. The seat sides and stretchers were shaped by laminating eight 1/8-in mahogany plies that were pre-bent and glued over a form. The seat sides were constructed of 3-in wide stock to achieve the taper that makes the seat back wider than the bottom. This shortened the dowel span in the seat bottom reducing the flex and strengthening the seat where the load is the greatest. Finally, all 94 dowel holes were drilled prior to shaping and the dowels glued in at the end.

Having to put in 200 hours or so before I could even sit in it was the hardest part of this project.

Ben Johnson

Ben Johnson | *Appalachian State University*

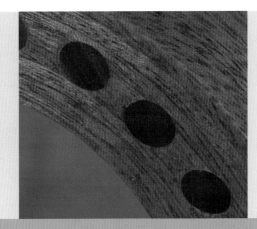

The main inspiration for my work is the use of dramatic angles and proportions. The goal of this project was to create a modern dining chair with ergonomic sensitivities, exaggerated proportions and traditional joinery. Measurements of differently-sized people and already existing chair back profiles were compiled to create the final profile of the back, to fit a wide range of body types.

The entire chair, except the front legs, is constructed from one 10 in by 12 ft piece of solid maple. The main challenge was to design the individual pieces to fit onto one piece of lumber.

Multiple jigs were created to assist in first and secondary CNC processes. Inserting cherry dowel pegs at the top and bottom of the back in conjunction with the connections to the frame prevented flexing. Multiple bolts were used for each slat to connect the back to the frame, and sturdy box joints to assemble the frame. The dining chair was hand sanded and finished in linseed oil, and upholstered with upholstery foam and micro fiber suede.

Matthew Harrell

Matthew Harrell | *Georgia Institute of Technology*

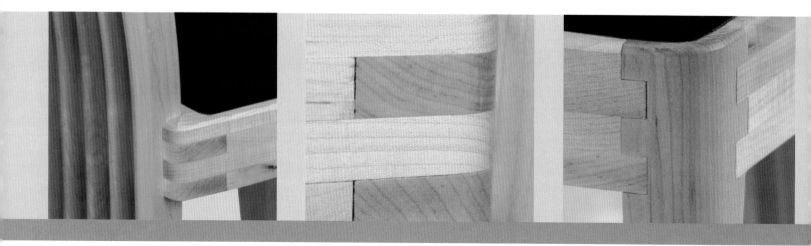

Creative | Chairs

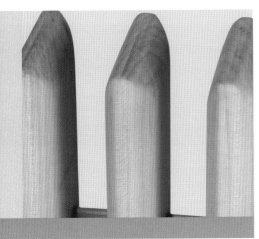

Contemporary Dining Chair

Traditional | Chairs

Newport
Corner Chair

My goal for this project was to closely (but not exactly) replicate the sculptural nature and excellent proportions of the original corner chair made for John Brown by John Goddard in Newport, Rhode Island circa 1780. The greatest challenge was creating the working drawings from two photographs and two dimensions of the original chair in Fine Points of Furniture, Volume II by Albert Sack.

I chose two air-dried cherry boards and paid careful attention to grain selection so that the strong grain of the cherry would harmonize with the compound curves within the design. I book-matched the ends of the arm, back spats and aprons to enhance the symmetry of the chair.

Traditional mortise and tenon construction was employed for all joints except at the front leg, where a pair of sliding dovetails adds strength. I carved the ball and claw feet with gouges and shaped the parts with spokeshaves and rasps.

A finish of shellac over oil, rubbed to a satin sheen, was applied to bring out the beautiful grain and natural color of the cherry. I had the seat professionally upholstered with leather.

Joshua Nickolds Williams

Joshua Nickolds Williams | *Rockingham Community College*

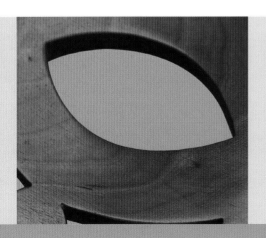

This wine rack was built of salvaged walnut and maple wood, but designed for use in a formal living or dining room setting.

Proper storage of wine bottles was considered in the design. A long, narrow opening in both the walnut top and cherry box directly below this area allow some of the labels on the bottles to remain visible. The removable, custom cutting block for cutting cheese was built from the remaining scraps of walnut and cherry.

The maple box appears to be floating separate from the legs and top due to a 1/4-in reveal between the different wood species. To create the reveal, a small "spacer" piece of wood was glued between each leg and the box. The use of screws or bolts was avoided for this connection in order to maintain a purity of form. Instead, dowel pins connect the legs to the top. Each of the twelve dividers that separate the wine bottles was hand planed and sanded to the perfect length so that it sat flush with the front edges of the box and fit snuggly into the routed grooves.

Kirsten Skinner

Kirsten Skinner | *Miami University*

Creative | Tables

Wine Rack

Creative | Tables

"My Feathered Friends" Demilune Table

Through my designs I hope to bring the delight, peace and tranquility of the outdoors to our modern indoor spaces. The bird motif on this table gives it a light and cheerful feel. The tabletop is an eight-section sunburst with four birds perched on branches.

I tried to make the birds as true to life as possible, and hope that viewers can identify the black-capped chickadee, the American goldfinch and the purple finch. The fourth bird is not readily identifiable and is bound to have birdwatchers consulting their field guides!

The front apron substrate is laminated bendable plywood, the legs and back apron substrates are poplar and the top substrate is MDF. All primary surfaces are veneered with bird's eye maple—the legs were veneered using a common household iron while the other parts were veneered using a vacuum press. The front leg is attached to the front apron with a bridle joint reinforced with two screws. The side legs are joined with the front and back apron with biscuits. The top is attached with metal z-clips. The table is finished with an oil/varnish blend.

Dan Overby

Dan Overby | *Rockingham Community College*

I believe that wood is most beautiful when the grain ripples through a carved or shaped surface, and that the highly carved, organic forms of art nouveau furniture are some of the most spectacular expressions of this ideal. So I chose to make a console table with art deco design elements, downplaying the arts and crafts-style coffee table of my class assignment.

To achieve the long, sinewy, elegant legs, a shallow arc was cut out of the two outside faces of each leg, then a contoured foot cut out of the bottom inside faces. I included an arced, double cloud lift motif on the front and rear aprons, contouring the design to look like stylized waves crashing. On my breadboard ends, I carved the "folded linen" motif I saw on a drawer pull.

The art deco elements of the table did not really coalesce until I stumbled upon the pattern for the stretcher—the double cloud lift motif from front and back aprons, with the cloud lift stepping "in." I created a routing jig and routed this pattern on three different levels.

All the carving and shaping was done with rasps, files, and rifflers—no chisels. The table is made entirely of solid American black walnut and finished with six coats of antique oil.

Scott Price

Scott Price | *Cerritos College*

Traditional | Tables

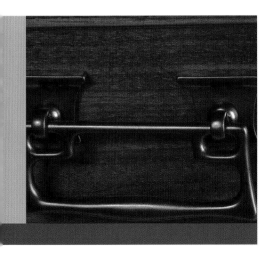

Art Deco Inspired Console Table

Mommy & Me Seating

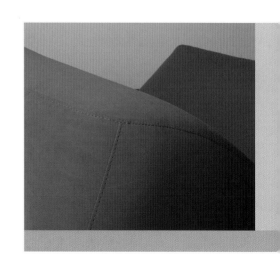

Mommy & Me seating addresses parent/child relationships. It provides a nurturing place for a parent and child to curl up together for shared activities such as reading or watching movies. Birds' nests and animal dens inspired an organic form with soft edges and uplifted sides.

The upholstery is a rubberized fabric that is stain resistant yet soft. The chair is raised off the ground on runners to protect little fingers and toes from accidents when rocking. It also has a niche for book storage.

Modeling the form in 3D allowed me to understand the shape and how to output sections of the form. I created the shape using a wood form to be covered by a layer of foam and upholstery. I modeled the form using 3D software and then cut virtual sections of the shape at 4-in intervals. These sections were cut with a CNC out of 1/2-in plywood and then screwed to a base cut from a preformed plywood radius. Lath was added across the sections. I then worked with a fabricator to cut the foam, and an upholsterer to cover it. The runners were created by bending oak strips.

Ana Luisa Franco

Ana Luisa Franco | *Art Center College of Design*

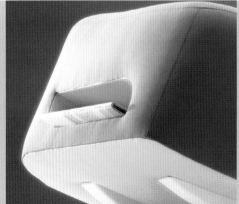

This lounge was born from an idea centered on simplicity, elegance and balance. The form is minimalist, refined to a delicate balance of rhythmic, flowing lines, and conveys a clear sense of tranquility. The goal was to create a piece that enhances the lounging comfort as well as the overall aesthetic of a space.

Considering ease of manufacturing, the concept relies on a single mold for its two main parts and contains no hardware. The primary form is reflected along a horizontal axis. Materials include: bendable birch plywood, white maple veneer, wenge supportive wedges and oak dowels. A 3-in bedding of TempurPedic foam wrapped in light chocolate faux suede rests on a finely developed curve that gracefully contours a broad scope of body types. With an optimum thigh-torso angle of 128 degrees, the lounge provides the user with excellent circulation.

Although intending to remain traditional, I wanted to express a style that is not so easily definable. Intended to remain somewhat neutral, yet distinguished, the design was styled to complement a variety of home environments. After a long day, the Horizon offers a warm, soothing experience to indulge in, guilt-free.

Hamilton Trimm

Hamilton Trimm | *Auburn University*

Traditional | Upholstered

Horizon

Propeller
Study Bench

This study bench was dictated by my studio apartment living constraints—a bench to also serve as a drafting table, with a storage shelf for study materials and a drawer for drafting supplies. The most time-consuming part of this design was hammering out the complicated proportions for a good-looking and compact, yet ergonomic multi-tasking bench.

I love the resiliency, feel and longevity of hardwoods, and specifically like to achieve harmony with contrasting wood types in a unified theme. I chose a highly figured cherry contrasted with the lightest wood available, Virginian white holly, with accents of tulip, a white and red striated exotic wood. The tulip forms the pencil rest and bottom of the drafting table as well as the unique joint in the bench surface that I call the propeller joint. The integration of clean aluminum doweled through the side aprons, pencil rest and revolving backrest also adds an attractive detail that seems to contrast sharply with the figured wood grain.

I finished the piece with multiple coats of boiled linseed and tung oil, and carnauba and beeswax. This creates a solid natural finish that is easier to repair and is more wholesome to the touch.

Tighe James Smalley

Tighe James Smalley | *Appalachian State University*

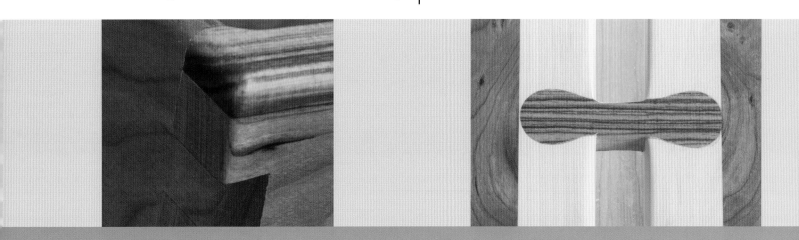

The Flex Shelf System is a fusion of two basic functions: storage and product mobility. I also don't like the idea of waste.

What if you could save time by keeping everything in a shelf organized, lightweight for transport, durable enough to withstand abuse and cool looking? My main goal was to eliminate the packing and unpacking process of shelf contents, as well as trying to discover a method to securely stack the shelf on top of another. So very simply, the shelves basically 'plug' on top of one another. The bottom portion has a female end and the top has a male end. The handles are made from the separation of the inner templates, thus making transportation effortless and uncomplicated.

The Flex form was designed in AutoCAD. Sheets of 1-in ultra-light MDF and 3/4-in construction grade plywood were then cut on a CNC machine and the templates laminated together. The snap-cover can be a variety of materials, such as dry erase board, chalkboard, polyethylene or ABS.

I'm inspired by the sensibility aesthetics and form of Japanese design, like Tadao Ando, Issey Miyake, Isamu Noguchi, and Hayao Miyazaki.

Jonathan Nazareth Zabala

Jonathan Nazareth Zabala | *Art Center College of Design*

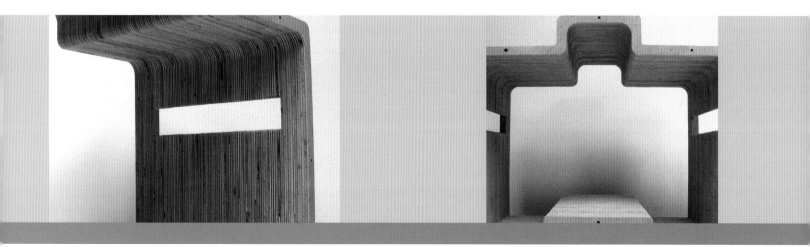

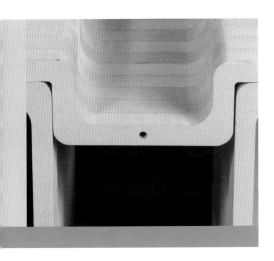

Flex
Shelf System

Team

Flex Folding Stool

Our stool design was informed by package designs from all over the world, since packaging necessitates light, attractive and collapsible design. Rather than approach design as a styling or formal exercise, we chose to design a stool that focused on multifunction and portability while at the same time addressing an economy of materials.

With manufacturability in mind, we carefully determined the AutoCAD CNC layout and router path for each component on a standard sheet. For instance, an 8 ft by 4 ft by 1/8 in Baltic birch plywood sheet yields 16 sides, producing 4 stools with 12 percent waste (tool path included). A 5 ft by 5 ft by 1/8 in plywood sheet yields 12 tops with 15 percent waste (tool path included).

Weighing only 5.47 lbs, the Flex Folding Stool can accommodate a variety of body types and sizes. The top is made of 1/8-in Baltic birch plywood of one-sided post-formed plastic laminate which allows the seat to flex.

This stool is ideal for individuals living in tight spaces or lofts. It folds flat and can be stored underneath a bed or couch, in the closet or even hung on a wall.

Mathew Birtch
Jessica Lertvilai

Mathew Birtch
Jessica Lertvilai | *Sheridan College*

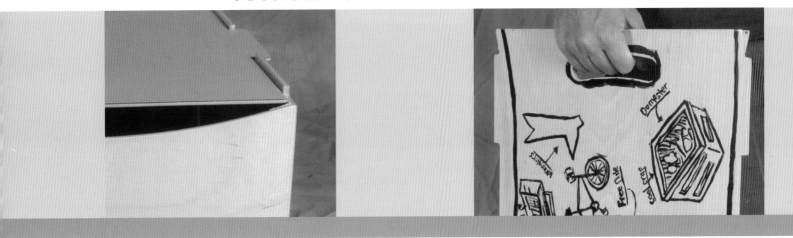

Detail "Lolli"

Casework-Cabinets – Creative

Holly Huff, Georgia Institute of Technology . . . . .Daisy Sideboard

James Kearl, Brigham Young University . . . . .Gumby's Coffin & Friend

Katie Stanchak, Georgia Institute of Technology . . . . .Television Stand

Rachel Winderweedle, Georgia Institute of Technology . . . . .Walnut Chest

Chairs – Creative

Whitney Bradford, Appalachian State University . . . . .Phyllis

Matthew Parks, Appalachian State University . . . . .The Klyde Rocker

Sarah Puchosic, Kansas State University . . . . .Links

Laura Swander, Auburn University . . . . .La Femme Chaise Lounge

Stephen M. Williams, University of Idaho . . . . .Treble Rocker

Chairs – Traditional

Skylar Davis, Appalachian State University . . . . .The EasySit Mission Recliner

Tables – Creative

Justin Barrett, University of Kentucky . . . . .pedro-z

Brittany Davis, Brigham Young University . . . . .Stainless Arc Entry Table

Matthew Hieb, Brigham Young University . . . . .Bridge Table

Tables – Traditional

April Jefferies, Kansas State University . . . . .TV's Last Stand

Julie Reese, Auburn University . . . . .The Marron Table

Matthew Blake Smith, Auburn University .Katana side Table

Upholstered – Creative

Heather Hulgan Knowles, Auburn University . . . . .Lolli

Special Theme – Special Needs Furnishings

Casey Kuffner, University of Kentucky . . . . .Toy Blocks

Brad Moreman, Auburn University . . . . .Home School

Detail "The Klyde Rocker"

Creative | Casework-Cabinets

Holly Huff | *Georgia Institute of Technology*

The Daisy Sideboard is RTA (ready to assemble) and almost every joint is held together with Häfele Solofixes. The holes were all predrilled when the plywood was machined, the joints were glued and the Solofixes used to register the parts and clamp down the joint.

The door details were conceptualized as a modern adaptation of the famous George Nelson Ball clocks of the 1950s.

Holly Huff

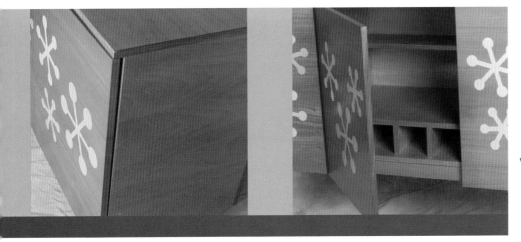

Daisy Sideboard

Creative | Casework-Cabinets

James Kearl | *Brigham Young University*

In order to provide the necessary strength for the suspended shelves, steel rods run through both sides of the shelf.

The concept started with a shelving unit that looked like it was growing out of the spot in which it was planted, a living thing stretching out of its confining box. The shelves are merely passing through, going wherever they wish.

James Kearl

Gumby's Coffin & Friend

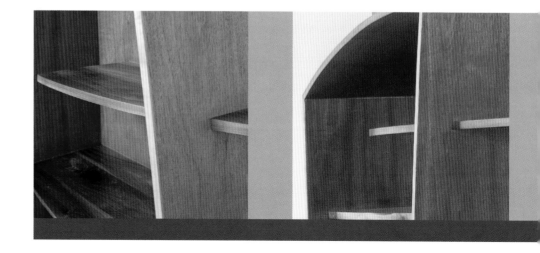

Creative | Casework-Cabinets

Katie Stanchak | *Georgia Institute of Technology*

All pieces were cut from two sheets of plywood with minimal waste. A total of eight parts are joined with Mini-Fix connectors and dowels. It can be assembled in less than 15 minutes with a screwdriver and a mallet.

Katie Stanchak

Television Stand

Creative | Casework-Cabinets

Rachel Winderweedle | *Georgia Institute of Technology*

This chest is constructed entirely of one piece of walnut-veneered plywood. Each piece of the chest was designed using AlphaCAM and then exported to a CNC router, where the individual pieces were cut.

The interior cavity of the chest remains unfinished to enhance the nostalgia of a hope chest.

Rachel Winderweedle

Walnut Chest

Creative | Chairs

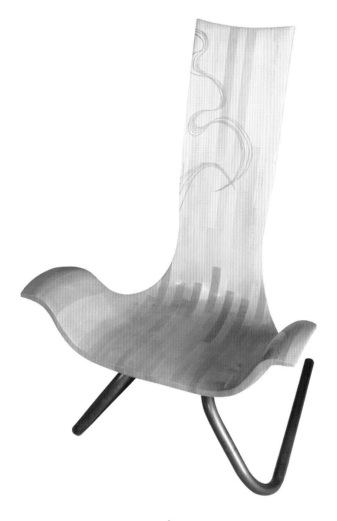

Whitney Bradford | *Appalachian State University*

Phyllis is a chair that is both visually and physically comparable to the soft, inviting comfort of an upholstered chair while still using the functionality of wood.

The turquoise design is to emulate the look of fabric. I call this concept 'wooden upholstery'.

Whitney Bradford

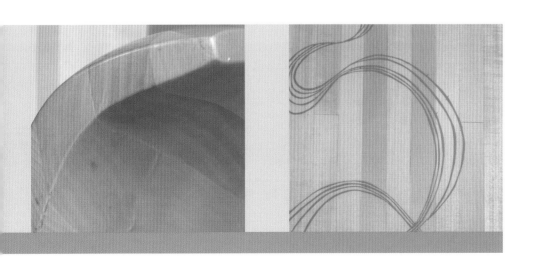

Phyllis

Creative | Chairs

Matthew Parks | *Appalachian State University*

Almost all of the shaping of the different pieces was done by hand with the use of a spokeshave, which gives the chair a sculptural quality.

All of the joints were chosen to create a chair that could bear the sitter's weight with minimal glue and no metal fasteners.

Matthew Parks.

The Klyde Rocker

Creative | Chairs

Sarah J. Puchosic | *Kansas State University*

The Links chair is a continuous, cost-effective, environmentally conscious alternative to an urban lawn chair. A design challenge was to make the chair adjustable between upright and lounge positions.

The chair was painted all white to express the concept of mass versus void.

Sarah J. Puchosic

Links

Creative | Chairs

Laura Swander | *Auburn University*

La Femme Chaise Lounge was inspired by the delicate feminine nature of working women, and their strength and durability in the workplace. This chair is specially made for women—it is more petite than most lounge chairs and is not overbearingly masculine.

There are no mechanized pieces or hardware in this chair, making the design easily manufactured.

Laura Swander

La Femme Chaise Lounge

Creative | Chairs

Stephen M. Williams | *University of Idaho*

Music plays a great role in my life and I wanted to design a piece that was not only relaxing like music, but also had flowing lines like a sweet melody.

The Italian poplar bendwood tended to be rather brittle. For fear of breakage from someone sitting on it, a skin of stronger birch plywood was laminated to each side, which greatly increased its strength.

Stephen M. Williams

Treble Rocker

Traditional | Chairs

Skylar Davis | *Appalachian State University*

I used Gustav Stickley's craftsman design as my starting point and then gave it a more modern look. To get a better feel for what people liked and didn't like, I used my class as a focus group.

The seat has a webbed bottom and a spring core, surrounded by 3-in foam and topped with 1-in memory foam.

Skylar Davis

The EasySit Mission Recliner

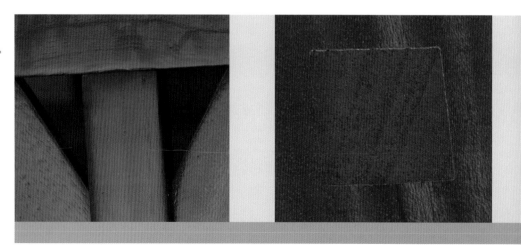

Creative | Tables

Justin Barrett | *University of Kentucky*

I find the "u" shape to be a very interesting form to work with since it has an implied inside and outside.

This nightstand is composed of 3/4-in MDF board and veneered with three different plastic laminates.

Justin Barrett

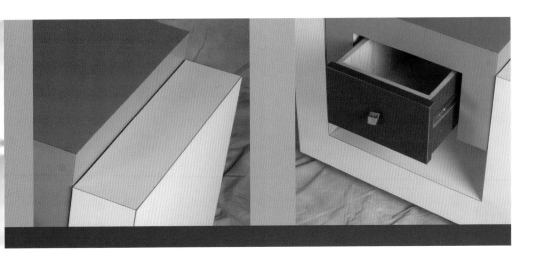

pedro-z

Creative | Tables

Brittany Davis | *Brigham Young University*

I wanted to create a sense of floating, lightweight and graceful space with this piece.

Curved cherry wood stretchers support the curved stainless steel sheet metal. A slit in the sheet metal allows the glass top piece to slide through and rest on the cherry stretchers. So the support system is hidden, creating the floating feel.

Brittany Davis

Stainless Arc Entry Table

Creative | Tables

Matthew Hieb | *Brigham Young University*

This bridge table is inspired by the arching spans of a bridge. Cues from Egyptian style are evident in the legs as they extend beyond the top of the table.

The stainless steel pivot-point was a visually interesting solution for joining the legs. Also, the outer legs can be removed and reinserted on the rods at a different angle to transform the table from an entry table to a coffee table.

Matthew Hieb

Bridge Table

Traditional | Tables

April Jefferies | *Kansas State University*

With advancing technology, all television components will soon be mounted on the wall. I wanted to create an attractive piece of furniture to accommodate the television of yesterday.

The shelves are supported by aluminum cross braces which are anchored in slots in the legs. These slots had to be made before the legs were turned in order to ensure accuracy.

April Jefferies

TV's Last Stand

Traditional | Tables

Julie Reese | *Auburn University*

The table was crafted using no hardware or foreign materials and each piece of wood still had the bark on it when I bought it.

The tabletop was made of three planks of ash wood, which were biscuit-joined together. The mortise to join the legs to the table had to be carefully chiseled to achieve the perfect square and a perfect fit.

Julie Reese

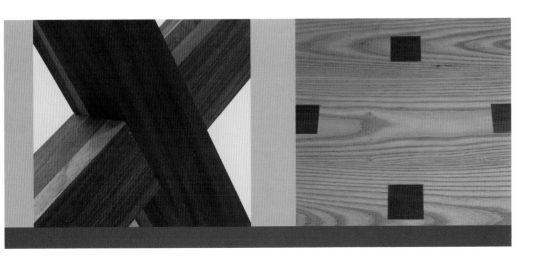

The Marron Table

Traditional | Tables

Matthew Blake Smith | *Auburn University*

Asian furniture and culture inspired this piece. Japanese swords, along with most Asian swords, have a slight curve to them—that's where I got my arches.

Construction used rough lumber along with wood glue, wedges, dowels, lap joints and biscuit joints. The walnut dowel joints are a special feature—I had to make them all.

Matthew Blake Smith

Katana Side Table

Creative | Upholstered

Heather Hulgan Knowles | *Auburn University*

By using rubber material for the squares, each part of the chair is reproducible by using a series of molds. I constructed three molds for the laminated veneer frame and one mold to cast the rubber.

The gracefulness and whimsy combined in Lolli create an elegant hostess suitable for a variety of environments.

Heather Hulgan Knowles

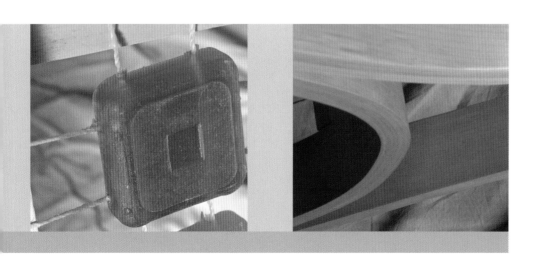

Lolli

Special Theme

Casey Kuffner | *University of Kentucky*

This work was inspired by the birth of my son.

My first building challenge was to make the boxes look as much like a toy as possible. So I hid the function of the piece–drawers, shelves and a toy box –by making all sides of the box a relief of a colored plastic laminate letter.

Casey Kuffner

Toy
Blocks

Special Theme

Brad Moreman | *Auburn University*

This desk was designed for the Good Samaritan Orphanage in Nairobi, Kenya, where the children share schoolroom and bedroom in the same space. It is designed to be suitable for education as well as a simple transition to a place to sleep.

Two issues were constant: children's safety and construction methods without power tools or special woodworking skills, in order for units to be produced by woodworkers in the orphanage.

Brad Moreman

Home School

Detail Table

"Rocking Airplane"

Casework-Cabinets – Creative

Johnny Karam, David Douglas High School . . . . .Quilted Blanket Chest

Josiah Whitney, Cedar Ridge High School . . . . .Waterfall Desk

Casework-Cabinets – Traditional

Vitaliy Verbovskiy, David Douglas High School . . . . .Craftsman Curio Cabinet

Nate King, Cedar Ridge High School .Curly Maple Nightstand

Myles Multhauf, Hartford Union High School . . . . .Eight-Drawer Mission StyleDresser

Chairs – Creative

John Maher, Princeton Day School . . . . .Contour

Tables – Creative

Trevor Herbst, David Douglas High School . . . . .Pedestal Table

Michael Hoff, David Douglas High School . . . . Leach Style Treadle Pottery Wheel

Tables – Traditional

Meredith Smith, Cedar Ridge High School . . . . .Shadow

Mary Van Dempsey, Cedar Ridge High School . . . . .Flitter

Special Theme – Special Needs Furnishings

Nate Cook, Bellaire High School . . . . .Rocking Airplane

Team Projects

Emily Kale and Charles Brannen,

Cedar Ridge High School . . . . .Puzzle Me Pretty

Hannah Maxwell and Michael Moore,

Cedar Ridge High School . . . . .Hot 'N Spicy

Quilted
Blanket Chest

I drew this chest from my idea of pressure forcing the sides to implode into the lid. I built the chest out of black walnut, maple and koa. The interior is lined with tongue-and-groove red aromatic cedar. The maple panels and the walnut around them are curved. To highlight the division between the lid and box, there are koa details at the bottom of each. There is a 30-degree tilt on the lid, which flows right into a domed top, which I hand rasped into shape. Two recessed handles are on the lid and I used a piano hinge along with two mortised side stays for support.

The panels are constructed out of wiggle wood and veneers. This was the most challenging aspect of this project. I had to add two pieces of Formica on the press to help even out the pressure, to apply the wiggle wood and veneers in the correct curve. The panels have a lacquer finish on them and the rest has been done in Sam Maloof's oil finish.

Johnny Karam

Johnny Karam | *David Douglas High School*

Exotic wood and figured woods give me great inspirations. Also, my admiration of curved pieces of furniture inspired me to build this desk.

The first parts I made were the curved panels on the inside of both of the bases. After mold-pressing a piece of 3/4-in kerf core with 1/4-in plywood on either side in the vacuum bag, I built the other parts of the two cases and assembled them together. Making the two adjacent sides of the case line up perfectly with the curved panel proved to be a significant challenge. Once I made the four case sides line up, I glued them together using biscuits.

I used a sapeli pommele veneer for the drawer fronts and a figured birch veneer for the sides of the cases with Spanish cedar borders. The table-top is made with a waterfall bubinga veneer and a maple border. Blum donated six pairs of full extension drawer slides with the Blumotion soft-close mechanism, which I used on the six drawers in this desk. The desk is finished with a sprayed on lacquer finish.

Josiah Whitney

Josiah Whitney | *Cedar Ridge High School*

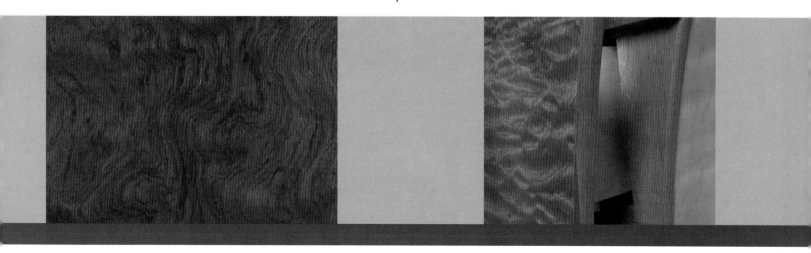

Creative | Casework-Cabinets

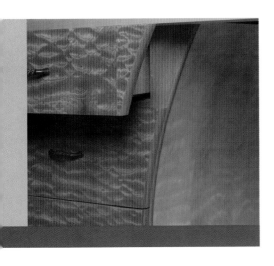

Waterfall
Desk

Craftsman Curio Cabinet

I designed this one-of-a-kind cabinet based on the traditional craftsman curio cabinet, and changed all sizes to fit modern conveniences.

I went all out on trying to have this cabinet last for a long time. I used haunch mortise and tenons to hold my project together. I thought it would add style and strength to my large design. I also decided instead of having the curio cabinet sit on the ground, I would have it stand at eye level. With that idea, I made the bottom portion the same design and improved the weight endurance with my arched base. To light up my cabinet, I used halogen round cabinet lights. The pulls and hinges are the same as they used in the craftsman era.

During this project, I learned many valuable lessons: I learned that everything must be just how you want it in order for you to be happy with what you're designing; I also learned that the finish of the wood is as valuable as the type of wood you use (quarter-sawn white oak).

Vitaliy Verbovskiy

Vitaliy Verbovskiy | *David Douglas High School*

Our class was assigned to build a nightstand planned by Blum. I used lyptus as a border for my top and for the legs. There is a curly maple veneer on the outside and maple veneer on the inside of the cabinet. The inlaid ebony, which is a diagonally placed square, mirrors the rectangular skeleton. I chose a streamlined design, which works very well and coordinates well with the hardware.

The plans were in millimeters and I had a lot of trouble adapting to the metric system, which made me have to redo the plans to compensate for the mistake I made in measuring. This was also the first time that I ever used veneer, and I found it quite challenging. The entire cabinet is RTA (ready-to-assemble) and uses hardware provided by Blum. The RTA fasteners for the case were installed using one of Blum's mini presses.

Despite the fact that it was a required assignment, I found a way to make it my own and I am very proud of the work I have done.

Nate King

Nate King | *Cedar Ridge High School*

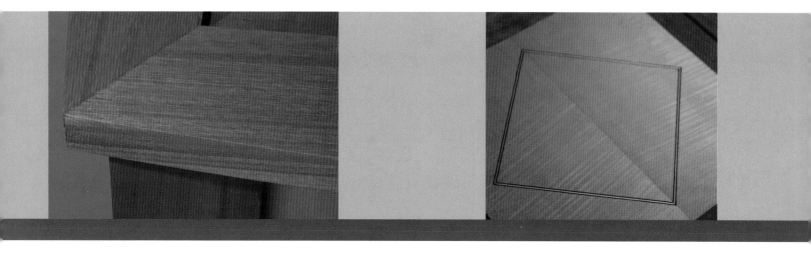

Traditional | Casework-Cabinets

Curly Maple Nightstand

Eight-Drawer Mission Style Dresser

My solid red oak dresser has many details, including ones visible on the inside, to make it classy and elegant. The box portion of the drawers is half-blind dovetailed (routered by hand) using 3/4-in black walnut, so the dovetailing is revealed when the drawers are opened. The six-piece drawers feature flush mount red oak fronts with full-extension, under mount slides. I sprayed the entire drawer box inside and out with lacquer to shine up the drawers. The solid red oak face frame has dovetailing joining from the inside, giving the front a bold solid look. The bottom rail has a subtle 1-in arc to add a classic line and element of distinction. The sides of the dresser are like a traditional panel door, with mortise and tenon joining the stiles and rails. The color is a wipe-on natural stain with a clear coat of lacquer.

I made a mirror framed in solid red oak to hang above the dresser. It has two brackets with a shelf on the top of it so that it is not just a plain frame with a beveled mirror in it.

This dresser is the final piece to complete my bedroom set.

Myles Multhauf

Myles Multhauf | *Hartford Union High School*

I designed this chair to mimic the contours of the human body while sitting in a comfortable position. I borrowed angles and measurements from an Adirondack chair I made a few years back, which was very comfortable.

The seat is made of eleven 2-in strips of maple—stacked sideways because I like the side grain of the wood. Every other piece is a different length to make a nice fingerjoint. From the back of the chair, you can see the wonderful contrast of the two different wood grains in the joint.

The legs are two arches made of quarter-sawn walnut veneer, glued and bent over a mold in a vacuum press. The legs are connected by two crosspieces, joined with tongue-and-groove, and pegged with two aluminum dowels. The seat is held in place on the legs by two pieces of aluminum dowel sticking a quarter of an inch out of the crosspiece, to hold it in perfect sitting position. The seat detaches from the arms, and the chair can be moved easily in two pieces.

I have been told that I have achieved my original goal of comfort without the use of pillows.

John Maher

John Maher | *Princeton Day School*

Creative | Chairs

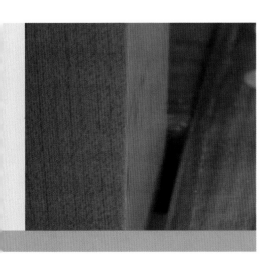

Contour

Pedestal Table

The concept of this table is a functional art piece that can be used every day. The wood I chose was 3/4-in American black walnut for all the pieces, except Baltic birch on the bottom of the drawer.

I started by making a mockup piece to show the strong and weak points within the arm. Then, starting from all rough wood, I squared up all the wood. Once the wood was the right size, shaping was the next step. Using the band saw I cut the pieces to the right shape. After that the pieces were put together to create the table. Last, but not least, I had to sand and put on the finish.

One of the main features in the construction are the bridle joints found on the legs and on the arm of the table. Gluing the bridle joints on the legs was a challenge because there were no flat surfaces to clamp together. It also took many attempts to glue on each leg one at a time. I hand carved the handle for the drawer and used rasps on the arm to create the beveled edge.

Trevor Herbst

Trevor Herbst | *David Douglas High School*

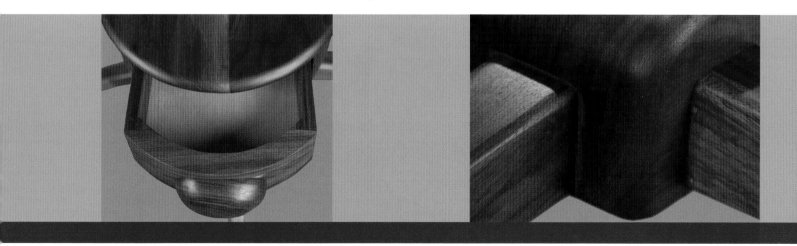

I started this project when my ceramics teacher asked me if I would be interested in building a foot treadle pottery wheel for him. I didn't have any plans to follow except a couple of drawings with a few specs on it. I had to design it, figuring out how it could be assembled and still be disassembled if needed. Not only did I have to design the woodwork but I also had to design the mechanics of the wheel so that it would work. The shelf on it was designed so that it could be easily put on and taken off without any fasteners. We decided to build it out of mahogany and maple, with accents of black walnut. The basin is lined with copper so that it will catch the water from throwing pots.

I did a lot of research on finishes that would be durable and waterproof. What I came up with was the same kind of finish that they put on gunstocks, so that the piece would last a long time while being used and still look nice. This is a type of conversion varnish with a catalyst.

Michael Hoff

Michael Hoff | *David Douglas High School*

Creative | **Tables**

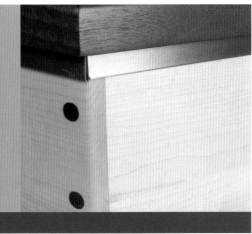

Leach Style Treadle Pottery Wheel

Shadow

The inspiration for this table came from a drawing I did earlier this year. My woodshop teacher had suffered a sudden, personal loss and took time away from school. On the card I made for him while he was away, I drew the original image for this tree. When he came back, he suggested that I recreate this tree in marquetry using the packet cutting technique. This piece reminds me of the small joys and beauties in the world, even in grief and loss.

The marquetry is five veneers, including walnut, walnut burl and cherry burl. I pressed it in the vacuum press over an MDF substrate. I surrounded the veneer with a maple border, which is the same wood as the base.

This is a simple leg and apron table, although I made the design more interesting and graceful by shaping the legs with a bandsaw and then flush pattern routing the aprons with a flush trim bit. The miters in the top have plate joinery, and the legs-to-aprons are mortise and tenon joints.

The legs were the biggest challenge. After bandsawing them I had to hand sand them, which was an incredible test of endurance and patience, even though I started with 40 grit.

Meredith Smith

Meredith Smith | *Cedar Ridge High School*

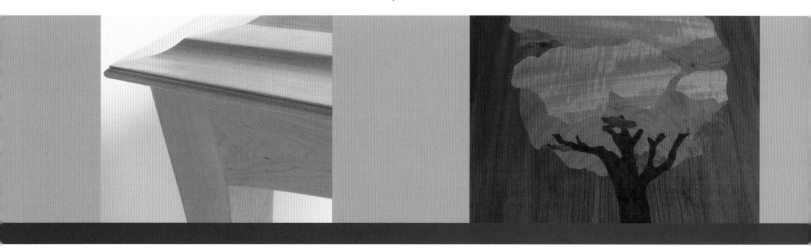

The inspiration for my table came from a quilt my grandmother made that has beautiful hummingbirds embroidered on the front.

I chose the basic leg and apron frame for my table, but added my own touches using veneer and tapering techniques and by adding a shelf. I chose to make my table of red oak because of the soft colors and beautiful medullary rays. The background for the marquetry on the top and the shelf is made of quartered lace wood veneer, which compliments the medullary rays on the front legs of my table. The hummingbird is made of sapeli, walnut, dyed koto (black) and remanufac-tured veneers. Both the shelf and the top have an MDF substrate balanced by a backer. Plate-jointed to the top is a solid red oak border with a routed edge.

The legs and aprons are held together using mortise and tenon joinery and the shelf is held in place using a groove cut in a smaller set of aprons. The top is fastened to the base using z-clips. Before attaching the top, I sanded the tabletop and base separately and then applied several coats of tung oil and wax.

Mary Van Dempsey

Mary Van Dempsey | *Cedar Ridge High School*

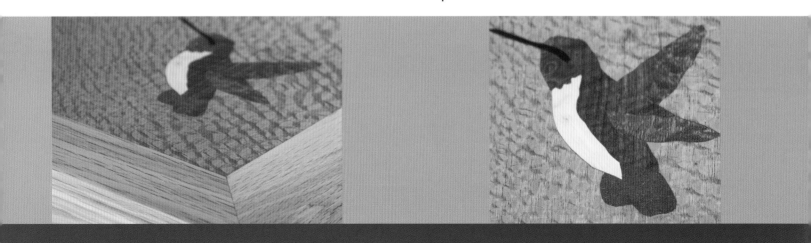

Traditional | Tables

Flitter

Rocking
Airplane

My woodworking class voted and decided to build a child's toy rocking plane. I had to think like a young child to figure out how a child would interact with this toy; what a child would find attractive; and safety factors to consider like sharp edges, points and screws. The design originated from student sketches, drawings, books, pictures, blueprints and brainstorming, and the final blueprints were compiled and constructed by the teacher.

Each part was traced from a stencil, cut out, sanded and painted. Then the finished parts were put together in an assembly line until all 30 of the planes were done. The multiple unique pieces required many different machines to build. For example, I used a bandsaw for the propeller and the lathe for the nose cone. While shaping the nose cones on the lathe, it was crucial to shape them so they looked alike. This was especially difficult because I shaped the nose cones all freehand with a chisel. I had to watch my own movements so I could copy them.

After completion, students took some of the planes home, some were sold to needy families and some were raffled off.

Nate Cook

Nate Cook | *Bellaire High School*

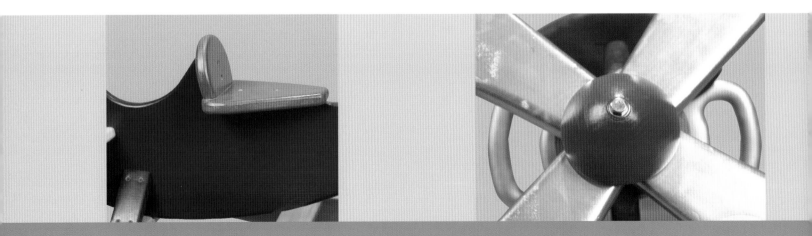

To build my table, I started with four boards of walnut for the legs: two became the square legs and the other two boards were cut from one corner to the other to create four triangular legs. The legs were joined to the walnut aprons using mortise and tenon joinery, making two triangular tables.

For the tabletop, I cut two triangles of particleboard and bordered the outer edges with 2-in solid walnut. I packet cut the veneer for the marquetry and glued it over the particleboard and walnut border. Then the outside edges of the tabletop were routed to reveal the walnut border underneath. Using the templates we cut on the CNC router, Charles flush-trimmed the long edge of each triangle to the puzzle pattern. We used ash to edgeband along the flush-trimmed edge and started sanding. The table was finished with a spray finish.

I am a first year woodworking student and had never used a router before. We had a very tight timeline and Charles, a third year woodworking student, added his skill and precision to help complete the base and to fit the puzzle tops.

Emily Kale
Charles Brannen

Emily Kale
Charles Brannen | *Cedar Ridge High School*

Team

Puzzle Me
Pretty

Hot 'N Spicy

Chili peppers are scattered all around our house. Be they cooking utensils, pictures or dried peppers in vases, my dad just loves peppers.

I used the technique of packet cutting to inlay 96 chili peppers onto MDF. The packet consisted of purpleheart, chili peppers of red-dyed koto and stems of maple, which I hand dyed using green RIT dye. Cutting out each individual pepper was extremely time consuming and tedious, yet I was overjoyed when I was finally able to put the top together.

The center of the tabletop is bird's eye maple, which I thought was a nice contrast with the purpleheart and the outside solid walnut border. The aprons of the table are solid maple. The legs on the table represent the shape and simplicity of a pepper, which were rather hard to cut out of the dense purpleheart material. These were cut on the bandsaw and then freehand routed.

I love working with veneer, yet despise the actual building process; whereas my partner who hates veneer and the design process, is an incredible builder. These complimentary skills made us a perfect match to build this project.

Hannah Maxwell
Michael Moore

Hannah Maxwell
Michael Moore | *Cedar Ridge High School*

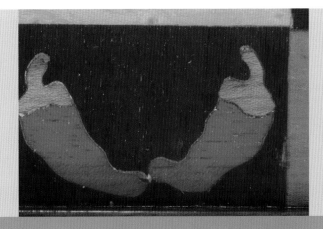

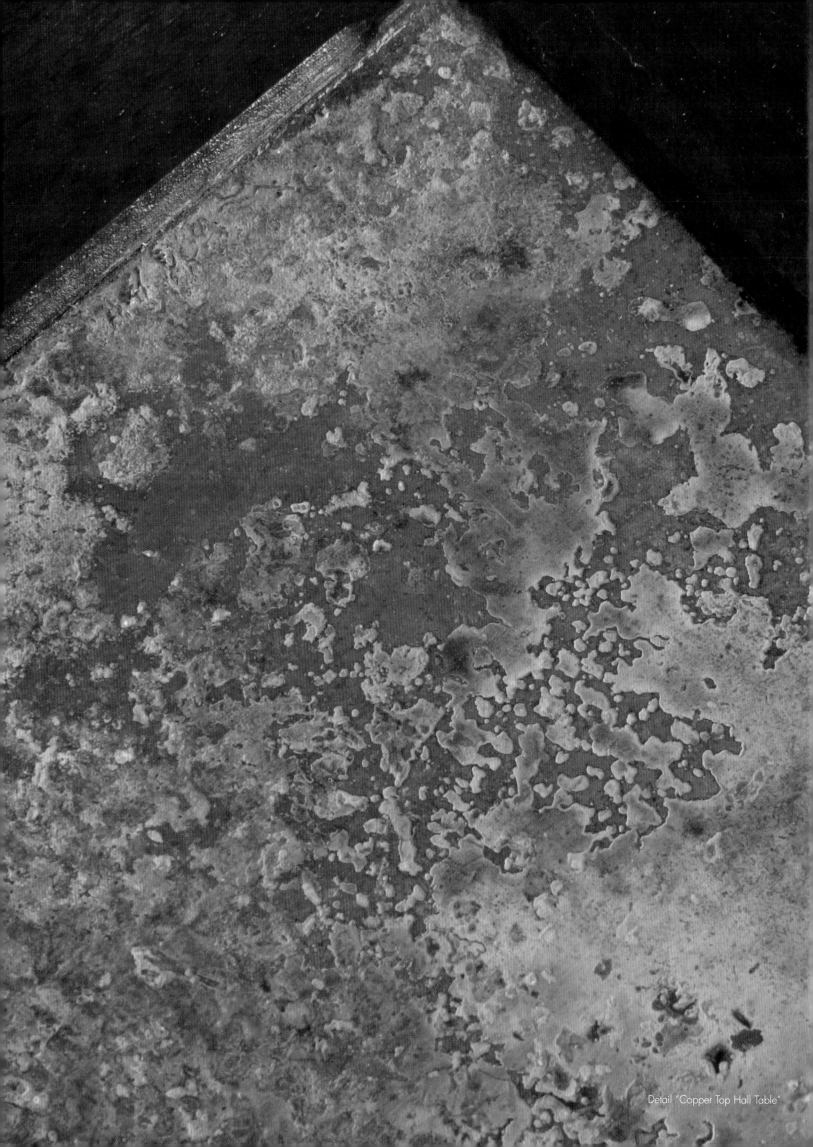

Detail "Copper Top Hall Table"

Casework-Cabinets – Creative

Efren Santiago, Jr., Cedar Ridge High School . . . . .Slumpy

Casework-Cabinets – Traditional

Tony Kurz, Porterville High School .Cherry and Maple Armoire

Jeffrey Michael Smith, Cedar Ridge High School . . . . .Purpleheart Nightstand

Tables – Creative

Clark Bristol, Princeton Day School . . . . .Table No.1

Cody James Hatfield, Jenkins High School . . . . .Chess Table

Hannah Maxwell, Cedar Ridge High School . . . . .A Gaze from a Window

Tables – Traditional

Maddie Baker, Cedar Ridge High School . . . . .Sunny Days

Jesse Garner, Jenkins High School . . . . .Copper Top Hall Table

Erin Ashley Rehm, Cedar Ridge High School . . . . .Erin's Beach Table

Detail "A Gaze from a Window"

Creative | Casework-Cabinets

Efren Santiago, Jr | *Cedar Ridge High School*

Seeing and watching a piece of furniture come together just makes me want to do it again and again.

I had some challenges with bending the wood for the top and side and working with the grain.

Efren Santiago, Jr

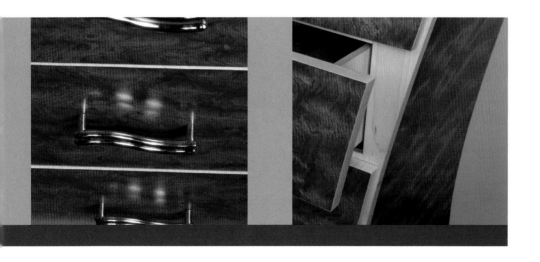

Slumpy

Tony Kurz | *Porterville High School*

We had to spray the lacquer on all the maple parts before assembly, because if we did not, the spots from the lacquer would show when we stained the cabinet. The inside has a large opening with partitions that hide the pocket doors, and plenty of room to house electronic components or clothing.

Tony Kurz

Cherry and Maple Armoire

Traditional | Casework-Cabinets

Jeffrey Michael Smith | *Cedar Ridge High School*

My piece is completely RTA (ready to assemble) and uses hardware provided by Blum. I modified the front doors to appear as if they are hidden and the left door has to be opened first.

This is the first time I used a spray-on finish with an HVLP (high-volume low-pressure) system.

Jeffrey Michael Smith

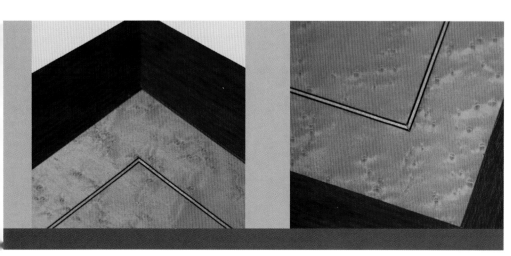

Purpleheart Nightstand

Creative | Tables

Clark Bristol | *Princeton Day School*

The bowl is made of plywood—originally rings—which I glued together. I smoothed the "steps" with a router on a semi-circular track and painful amounts of sanding.

The aluminum tubing is an unusual design feature. These metal supports are aluminum tubing around carriage bolts, which go into threaded inserts – three on each of the four legs.

Clark Bristol

Table No.1

Creative | Tables

Cody James Hatfield | *Jenkins High School*

This fancy chess tabletop was constructed out of alder and paduak squares with an ash border. Strips of paduak wood are inlayed vertically down the side of every leg.

I used a machine called the plasmaCAM to cut the 1/4-in sheet metal for the metal art integrated into the project, which brings out the color of the wood.

Cody James Hatfield

Chess Table

Creative | Tables

Hannah Maxwell | *Cedar Ridge High School*

The legs are created with six thin strips of walnut, which we had to pull around a form.

The idea for this table came to me one day when it was pouring down rain and quite a gloomy day. I was greatly longing to sit on our porch in the mountains and look out over a sunset.

Hannah Maxwell

A Gaze from a Window

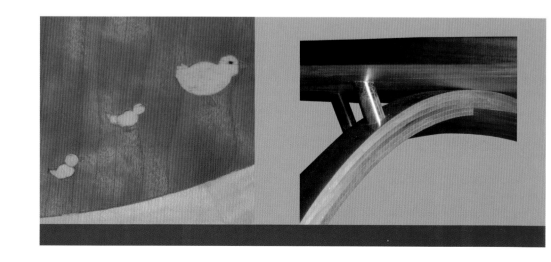

Traditional | Tables

Maddie Baker | *Cedar Ridge High School*

When I designed my table I wanted the deep, dark, café look, which I was able to find in walnut wood.

The legs and aprons are put together with a mortise and tenon joint, which I found rather challenging to do, as this was the first time I ever used any of the shop tools.

Maddie Baker

Sunny Days

Traditional | Tables

Jesse Garner | *Jenkins High School*

It was a challenge to get the copper to change colors the way I wanted and to fill the whole sheet of copper. I put a quarter of an inch of fine sawdust on top of the copper. Then I sprayed chemicals on the sawdust, wrapped the copper up in plastic and stored it away for a few weeks.

Jesse Garner

Copper Top Hall Table

Traditional | Tables

Erin Ashley Rehm | *Cedar Ridge High School*

To build this table, I had to learn how to use all the different machines, such as the tablesaw, radial arm saw, miter saw, mortiser, planer, jointer and various others.

The support bars on the underside of the table also serve as a footrest.

Erin Ashley Rehm

Erin's Beach Table

For many years, the high school woodshop program had received a negative connotation as a repository of students who didn't know what they wanted to do. It had also become the home of difficult-to-teach students. Yet there are more and more students who truly love working with wood.

Much of the credit has to go to the forward thinking leadership and support of groups such as AWFS®, to projects such as their design competition—the only national design contest that includes high school students—and to the publishing of the *Fresh Wood* series of books.

Why? There is absolutely no doubt that a national design competition and recognition are by far the best mechanisms to stimulate the juices of our young students. But developing the sincere interests and producing recognized results of our best and brightest creative minds requires the sustained challenge  and the earned respect of our educators. In other words, it requires a genuine team approach.

While a national event might achieve this, the job would only be half done if some sort of achievements record and recognition were not also produced. And this is where *Fresh Wood* plays such an important role. From a WoodLINKS USA perspective, the *Fresh Wood* publication has become a permanent fixture in all of their programs. Teachers use the book as a challenge to stimulate the creative thinking of those students who would otherwise just build hobby projects such as breadboards. *Fresh Wood* has set the national benchmark of wood-based projects built in entry-level skills programs: projects and ideas must be bettered in order to win future events.

Most important, the competition and *Fresh Wood* have provided the students and teachers with a permanent reminder and recognition of their achievements. This human touch is what counts and why our wood industry must continue to support these competitions, our schools, our students and the WoodLINKS program.

Steve Ehle has been a member of the editorial team of *Wood Digest* since 1986, and currently serves as Editor-in-Chief. Steve is also the state of Wisconsin coordinator of WoodLINKS USA and is widely seen as a champion voice for wood industry education.

WoodLINKS USA has become a resounding success across the United States. It has been offering its training and education program in the United States for more than five years, and has grown to more than 60 participating high schools. There are also two postsecondary schools participating in WoodLINKS. More than 125 students will receive their WoodLINKS certificates this year.

The national program averages about one new WoodLINKS school per month, and boasts more than 75 industry manufacturing partners who provide guidance and financial support to the WoodLINKS schools in their regions.

Also, a number of national and state associations, as well as some industry suppliers are assisting WoodLINKS. Just some of them are the Woodworking Machinery Industry Association, Trade Shows Inc., National Association of Store Fixture Manufacturers, Association of Woodworking & Furnishings Suppliers®, Wood Machinery Manufacturers of America, Architectural Woodwork Institute, Wood Component Manufacturers Association, International Woodworking Fair, Microvellum, Wagner Electronic Products, Franklin International and others.

**An Industry
Education Partnership**

HIGH SCHOOLS

Bellaire High School
204 West Forest Home Avenue
Bellaire, Michigan 49615
(231) 533-8141
www.bellaire.k12.mi.us
Students' instructor: Dave Barresi

Cedar Ridge High School
1125 New Grady Brown School Road
Hillsborough, North Carolina 27278
(919) 245-4000
www.orange.k12.nc.us/crhs
Students' instructor: Keith Yow

David Douglas High School
1001 SE 135 Avenue
Portland, Oregon 97233
(503) 261-8300
http://ddhs.ddouglas.k12.or.us
Students' instructor: Doug Ivey

Hartford Union High School
805 Cedar Street
Hartford, Wisconsin 53027
(262) 673-8950
www.huhs.org
Students' instructor: Jason Kraus

Jenkins High School
E. 702 Lincoln
Chewelah, Washington 99109
(509) 935-8671
www.chewelah.k12.wa.us/jhs
Students' instructor: Kevin Kernan

Porterville High School
465 West Olive Avenue
Porterville, California 93257
(559)793-3400
www.portervillehigh.nu
Students' instructor: Tim Newby

Princeton Day School
P.O. Box 75, The Great Road
Princeton, New Jersey 08542
(609) 924-6700
www.pds.org
Students' instructor: Aren Irwin

POSTSECONDARY SCHOOLS

Appalachian State University
Boone, North Carolina 28608
(828) 262-2000
www.appstate.edu
Students' instructor: Bill Hanner

Art Center College of Design
1700 Lida Street
Pasadena, California 91103-1999
(626) 396-2200
www.artcenter.edu/furniture
Students' instructor: David Mocarski

Auburn University
Department of Industrial Design
207 Wallace Center
Auburn Alabama 36849-5121
(334) 844-2364
www.auburn.edu/ind
Students' instructor: Tin-Man Lau

Brigham Young University
265 CTB
P.O. Box 24206
Provo, Utah 84602
(801) 422-4636
www.byu.edu
Students' instructor: Kip Christensen, Ph.D.

Cerritos College
11110 Alondra Boulevard
Norwalk, California 90650
(562) 860-2451
www.cerritos.edu
Students' instructor: Mike Jones

**Fox Valley Technical College
– Oshkosh Campus**
S.J. Spanbauer Center
3601 Oregon Street
P.O. Box 2037
Oshkosh, Wisconsin 54903-2037
(920) 424-0747
www.fvtc.edu
Students' instructor: Gerald Finch

Fullerton College
321 East Chapman Avenue
Fullerton, California 92832
(714) 992-7590
www.fullcoll.edu
Students' instructor: Tim Harrison

Georgia Institute of Technology
College of Architecture
247 – 4 Street
Atlanta, Georgia 30332-0155
(404) 894-3880
www.coa.gatech.edu
Students' instructor: Alan Harp

Kansas State University
Department of Interior Architecture &
Product Design
203C Seaton Hall
Manhattan, Kansas 66506
(785) 532-6011
www.ksu.edu
Students' instructor: David Brown

Miami University
501 East High Street
Oxford, Ohio 45056
(513) 529-1809
www.miami.muohio.edu
Students' instructor: John Weigand

Rockingham Community College
P.O. Box 38
Wentworth, North Carolina 27375
(336) 342-4261
www.rcc.cc.nc.us
Students' instructors: Art Pentz, David Kenealy,
Mike Quinn

Sheridan College
Furniture Studio, Trafalgar Campus
1430 Trafalgar Rd.
Oakville, Ontario L6H 2L1
Canada
(905) 845-9430
www.sheridaninstitute.ca
Students' instructor: Michael Elmitt

University of Idaho
College of Letters, Arts, & Social Sciences
Admin 112, PO Box 443154
Moscow, Idaho 83844
(208) 885-6426
www.uidaho.edu
Students' instructor: Jay Pengilly

University of Kentucky, College of Design
117 Pence Hall
Lexington, Kentucky 40506-0041
(859) 257-3030
www.uky.edu
Students' instructor: Len Wujcik

"'My Feathered Friends' Demilune Table

FRESH WOOD

Fresh Wood can be ordered online at www.mitrapublishing.com

For phone, fax or mail-in orders, contact Mitra Publishing Group

225 North Lima Street, Suite 6

Sierra Madre, California 91024

t. (626) 836-5506 f. (626) 836-5500

info@mitrapublishing.com

Special pricing is available for orders of 25 or more.

Fresh Wood makes a memorable gift for key customers, vendors and employees. You can even have your company logo imprinted on the book jacket to personalize this special gift. A minimum order of 10 copies is required for customized covers.
Call (626) 836-5506 for more information.

Bookstores and Libraries:
Discounts are available for Libraries and booksellers.
Books for resale can be purchased directly from Mitra Publishing Group, or from Baker & Taylor. Go to www.btol.com for information.